Fishing for Eternity

Fishing for Eternity

Poems from the River of Life

KENT GRAMM

RESOURCE *Publications* • Eugene, Oregon

FISHING FOR ETERNITY
Poems from the River of Life

Copyright © 2024 Kent Gramm. All rights reserved. Except for brief quotations in critical publications or reviews, no part of this book may be reproduced in any manner without prior written permission from the publisher. Write: Permissions, Wipf and Stock Publishers, 199 W. 8th Ave., Suite 3, Eugene, OR 97401.

Resource Publications
An Imprint of Wipf and Stock Publishers
199 W. 8th Ave., Suite 3
Eugene, OR 97401

www.wipfandstock.com

PAPERBACK ISBN: 979-8-3852-2295-7
HARDCOVER ISBN: 979-8-3852-2296-4
EBOOK ISBN: 979-8-3852-2297-1

05/23/24

*There the glorious Lord will be unto us
a place of broad rivers and streams.*

—Is. 33:21

"The Governor and his Council faintly remember the pond, for they went a-fishing there when they were boys; but now they are too old and dignified to go a-fishing, and so they know it no more forever. Yet even they expect to go to heaven at last."

—Henry David Thoreau, *Walden*

Contents

Trout Brook	1
The Rattle Bridge	5
Sunfish	8
The Tavern	10
Trout	13
The Ice	16
Yellow Perch	18
The Compleat Angler	24
thou shalt break them with a rod of iron	26
Pool (Doubt)	28
St. Croix	29
The Old Toll Bridge	32
The Town	36
The Northern Pike	37
The Worm	40
Bass: An Ode	44
The Beauty Spot	46
Gone Fishin'	48
"Here lies one whose name was writ in water."	50
Art and the Big Dam	51
Muskie	55
The Ocean	59
The Little Dam	62
Ballad of the Snakehead Fish	65
Old Fishermen	70
Fishing Pals	72

Indolence	74
Willow River Cemetery	77
The Willow River at Night	81
The Willow River in Heaven	90
The North Hudson Bridge	92

Trout Brook

He went before the mourning doves were up,
before sleep's vast, uncautious remembering
entirely diffused in daylight, one cup
of yesterday's coffee sipped cold for luck
standing at the stove and still remembering,
thinking of her who knows when, what moment
surfaced the deep mind's stream, what pool or eddy
caught a cast of sunlight—nothing chosen,
just life, come back in a dream from the dead:
his bride years ago back home, his chosen
Ingeborg, the lady who married a blacksmith—
his life's sole, incomparable, and sorrowful gift.

Probably not for luck he drank it cold:
his grandson would wake if he lit the stove,
or the aroma of its warmth would bring
her back more. The sleeping boy was rolled
in a blanket, suffering with his own
happy dreams, in the lightening little living
room that Martin chose to walk through although
he could have gone out the back porch. One look
at the boy. He meant Ingeborg was real.
Wading shoes, flyrod, lunch packed in his creel,
Grandpa opened the front door like a holy book;
closed it like a rainbow feeling for a small hook.

Martin walked the long dawn walk to Trout Brook
with Ingeborg, as they did in Norway
where he'd fish for salmon with golden hooks
and their life was one sunlit dawning day.
You could see the mountains from the stream's side
where they fried glittering fish in the unending
noon; and before them the afternoon—more
whole than the ocean, longer than the sky—
rested in their hands like a strained and bending
rod levering a silver fish to shore.
Now he walked along the little trout stream, and she
beside, the way she used to be, a walking dream.

As cool as morning was, he waded in;
and like an old time soldier he opened
the lidded cup of perforated tin
at his belt, his kind of ammunition,
the fisherman's most reliable friend:
worms. The rich Americans fished with flies,
encased themselves in rubber wading boots,
false-casted back in syncopated time—
hung up in bushes, limbs, and washed-out roots.
An immigrant thinks for himself, figures them out:
the rich come home with lies but he comes home with trout.

If flies were meant for fish they wouldn't fly,
they'd burrow through the earth and fall with crumbling
soil into the streams and be swallowed up
as death is swallowed up in victory—
or so the Holy Bible and the Pastor
had said on that muffled day when Martin held
their younger daughter in his arms and quelled
his sobs enough to say, "Look at Mother,
Lula, now, for you will never see her
again." And there she lay without a soul.
Lula didn't understand what she was seeing.
Ruth did: "Beauty is its own excuse for being."

Now sad Ruth's boy lay sleeping. Ruth had seen
her mother twice, but Martin had never—
or rather, once, and that continually,
for to love once is to love forever.
But the boy had heard his grandfather go,
had heard the quiet step and gentle door;
he heard the mourning dove, the kitchen clock,
the turning of the unreturning lock.
Every year he understands Martin more.
What his grandfather knew, he thinks he knows:
Beauty is the water where the heart's reflection swims.
There is a river even in Jerusalem.

My Ingeborg walks a stream of pure light.
The lady Martin knew I never knew,
but she is in my stream of blood, my life,
and I imagine her. We see the bright
reflection of the mind, silver on blue—
but see where he stands, in Trout Brook, narrow
stretch of a larger river called the Willow,
that enters the St. Croix where Malilieu,
so-called, empties toward the Mississippi,
which flows into the circling Seven Seas.
So Martin was a Mississippi man, Viking
of the Ganges, and the origin of things.

He's caught a pair of trout and laid them side
by side on fresh-torn grass in the cool dark
of his creel. Sadly alive, their gills rise
and fall like the lifting of a tired tide.
He knows we are not saved by our good works,
but something is. He kneels in the brook, pries
the creel's stiff lid and dips the basket in.
At dinner there will be an empty dish,
but he knows what his grandson imagines,
and a trout's no imaginary fish.
This morning he went fishing for eternity,
and cast his line into that ancient wine-dark sea.

The Rattle Bridge

The way that was the way is not the way—
the little iron bridge across the upper
Willow, in a narrow and secluded place,
fifty feet and one car width in the days
when still in use. Now called the Rattle Bridge,
it shook with every one of Grandpa's steps,
rusty and going nowhere: the small ridge
upstream carried the new span, all concrete,
and the modern road. Broad-pillared New Bridge
was no place to fish: too high, and no frets
and stops to rest your arms on; incomplete
but going somewhere, that's for sure. A street

out in the country, is what it felt like—
street to nowhere. Any good Lutheran
prefers the old way to the new; so do
the fish. The Rattle Bridge still stood rooted
in the river—structure for trout, bass, pike,
but mostly perch and all the kinds of sunfish:
bluegills, pumpkinseeds, and crappies. Dangle
a worm there awhile, and that's what you'd get:
sunfish, unless the little perch angled
you for your worm. The old way's a good bet,
the old timers said. Martin's grandson wet
his first line there; and he promptly tangled

it up inside that old bait casting reel—
the heavy black thread snarled in a bird's nest
that wound tighter the more he tried to free
it. The bobber hung in the air, at rest
forever it seemed. What's impossible
for a boy can be done by a woman,
so Signe, who had raised the boy to five
when tuberculin Ruth again fell ill
and now took care of the half-blind Martin,
took the boy's reel in hand. She could unbind
anything. She made the boy Norwegian
to his soul, an instinctive Lutheran

who spoke with her accent. And he still does
decades later. Now the old bridge is gone,
and the New Bridge is gone; but what was, was;
and even though he is standing there alone
after all these years where the trembling way
used to pause on the Willow, each end shaded
by summer trees—even though dismayed
by the blankness of everything, no roads
here any more, knee-high weeds to be waded
even to reach an airy standing place,
they were here. The river knows what it knows.
The way that was the way is where he goes.

What are we but the accent we have learned,
the shifting two-way road of memory,
and the bridges laid out by who knows who?
Some bridges can never be burned,
and some roads are like rivers.
Martin couldn't see or hear well that year,
and it only got worse. Signe's strong hands
trembled more and more with Parkinson's Disease.
The grandson doesn't know wisdom from beer
when it comes to what his reason understands,
and no ghosts come to give his old heart ease.
But it's always the river, always the river.

The river rhymes with itself and that's all.
There are no readers of a river, only
those who pass the fingers of their eyes across
the lights reflecting off its surface, going
their own way even though they chose to float
along the lines of time's gradual fall
to the sea. The river takes its own way
and nothing else takes it, and no one knows
the river but the river, and the river
is water whose knowing is its going.
The way that is the way is not the way.
It is the river, always the river.

Sunfish

Fish of seemingly endless fruitfulness
    and child, so named, of the full summer sun,
how the sunfish blesses our humbleness.
    Remember how the freckled boys would run
like schools of sunfish themselves, their crisp straw
    hats half-lifting under their pressing hands,
        clasping willow poles with swinging corks, feet
    bare and dusty, boyhood's own Americans
racing each other to the fishin' hole?
What's childhood but the unimagined soul
    in love with every happiness it meets?

Boys and girls want sunfish, little fighters—
    multitudes of always willing jewels
pretty as dreams unwrapped of Elder Night
    and plump in the hand: pumpkinseeds, bluegills,
dripping fresh water and sparkling silver, blue,
    yellow, orange, and red. They make you think
        God must be everywhere because they are,
    and all is well. Drop hook, line, and sinker
into that opaque blue of old belief;
drop age's infirmities and its grief—
    and answers come up glittering like stars.

How often we have lifted them like gypsy
    acrobats to a bridge's rusty rail
or reeled them in hard by their eggy lips
    to a grassy shore and a hazy pail
or a stringer where they breathed like sad fans—
    suffering indignities like children
        so we can always retrieve our first dream
    of summer. We can always be again
the first and last uncursed American,
a string of sunnies dangling from our hand,
    bare feet green beside the grassy mill stream.

The Tavern

The aging couple Jo and Andy still
ran their tavern a few miles from the old
rusty Rattle Bridge. A curve in the road:
a dozen houses, a forgotten mill,
and a general store made the less than hamlet
of Burkhardt, whose heart was Jo and Andy's
Tap. They lived above and behind the bar
and it was open all day, one of them
always there, usually Jo. "Oh him?"
she'd say. "He's gone fishin'. He took the car
so I'm stuck here anyway. What'll it be?"
Signe had a Pabst Blue Ribbon, Martin
a Leinenkugel with a shot poured in
or left on the side. Then she'd look at me.

Maybe she'd lean her weight on an elbow.
"And what about the quiet fisherman,
the young man?" Maybe she'd wipe her hands
on her apron, look at Signe. "You know,
you got a good boy." "*Ja*, he's a good boy,
Yo." Jo would reach across the bar and touch
Grandpa's shoulder. "Martin, do you know what?"
He would look up and she'd raise her strong voice:

"You got a good grandson there, Martin!" Staring
somewhere past her he'd say, "*Ja,*" then stop
and drink his beer. As if I were a man
she'd ask, "What can I set up?" "Orange pop,
please," and she'd always come back carrying
glass over bottle, and in her free hand

a Kit-Kat candy bar. "Thank you very
much," I'd say. "I like a well-mannered boy,"
she'd tell Signe. "And the Kit-Kat's on me.
You know, the boy don't look too good today."
"*Ja,* vell you know his uncle Louis died,
is vut it is." That day Jo quietly sighed
and limped away to bring another Kit-Kat
bar. "Here, son," she said, her big voice quiet.
Signe told me, "They had a little tyke,
once." Days when Signe's husband Art, a farm
hand, got off work and came along, he'd ask,
"Where's Andy fishin' today, Yo?" "Too warm
for the Rattle Bridge, he said. Way up past
New Richmond there's a little lake he likes."

Back in their younger days Andy and Jo
had pasted little signs behind the bar.
"We have a deal with the bank. They sell no
beer; we lend no money." "I'm not a slow
bartender. I'm not a fast bartender.
I am a half-fast bartender." It took
twenty years for the boy to get that one.

There were more than the boy can remember,
which is the case with any hieroglyphs,
revelations, sacred teachings inscribed
on the water of a happy childhood,
from which you come into maturity
diminished and trailing clouds of glory.
We don't remember heaven as we would.

Jo had curly black hair and river blue eyes.
She was eighty years and the hair was dyed,
but the eyes were true, and whoever saw
them lived forever, and kept his wishes.
She rubbed her crooked hands
like mythic magic lamps.
If you received a gift from them,
you never thirsted again.
When she pulled the tap, out came living water,
clear as justice, pure enough for pale fish
to inhale and turn to dryads, angels,
upanishads. God loves Andy and Jo;
now they serve saints free what they used to sell.
A boy can't prove it, of course, but he knows.

Trout

And God said, "I will make one thing perfect,
but one thing alone, lest creation forget
its maker." And God called forth the Elect,

who had repented like dogs, but no pet
strikes God as perfect. So God tried again,
brooding on the soup of nothing as yet,

and searching His mind for what to invent.
Imagine the grandeur of that. You can't.
The most humble of beings, most intent,

loving, God can make anything He wants.
Form. Perfection arises out of form.
As if with a partner, as if with chance,

God agreed to form. The sun became warm
and burst with light! Physics, mathematics,
eurythmics, and Indra's golden arms

came forth. Stars' exploding courses were fixed;
on Earth rivers were freed from their hydrogen
ball, and mountains rose from their granite fist.

It all looked pretty good. But perfection?
That's another story. Remember, one
thing only would be perfect. Beside sin,

nothing's here for it's own sake. Every stone,
every mayfly, every debutante's pout,
supports that perfection, is nothing alone.

Perfection, of course, is the species called trout,
salmoniae in the language of angels
(its own music transporting what is pronounced)—

one subspecies above all: the rainbow,
oncorhynchus mykiss—a lovely name,
so sweetly romantic. Only they know

(the angels, I mean) how this beauty came
to earth with all the long-jawed, spiked, walleyed
monstrosities beneath the pearly waves.

The trout is perfect: in form, how refined;
in temperament, noble—contemplative,
fierce, its integrity uncompromised

by fashions worn by wading fishermen;
in grace—oh, how to find words for its leap!
In intellect, cunning, shrewdness, acumen

unequalled; but most of all in beauty—
colour, flavour, deft elegance of shape,
yet beyond the numbered sum of these:

regal as the starry heavens, could take
its place on the last feast's mirrored plate—
as symbol of grace, incomparably great.

The Ice

My Lord, how he could stand out on the ice
all day at eighty. What would Martin say,
I wonder, about heated huts? Not nice,
I'm sure, with the cold bluntness of Norway—
if he'd bother to say anything at all.
These days they sit by machined holes
drinking beer and watching pro basketball,
substituting fish locators for souls—
driving out on the ice in pickup trucks
or gasoline-swallowing SUV's
and driving home to their wives stupid drunk.
Ice fishing is not what it used to be.

And I praise the Lord for that and say Amen.
It shows fishermen have learned how to pray.
The first time I went fishing with Martin
on the ice, I met him about mid-day
out on The Pond, where he'd been since morning.
I froze my ass, and wanted to get away
after an hour, and did—with his warning
unspoken in my soul—nothing he'd say
aloud, but clear. You will never add up
to anything but a preacher or banker
if you can't stand it out here. Your mother
raised you to be good, and you should thank her

by acting like a solid Norwegian.
At first I tried to confirm prophecy
by pretending to be a holy man
studying for the modern ministry,
but it was no go. Churches are fishing
shanties now, electronics out the wazoo—
entertainment centers and warm wishing
wells. Whatever is cozy can't be true.
It's Sunday: I could be evangelical,
singing praise songs monotonous as vice—
"A Hundred Bottles of Beer on the Wall,"
new version. It's better here on the ice.

Yellow Perch

"Some say that dreaming is but another form of waking."
—Brihadaranyaka Upanishad

The yellow perch is a small fish. Only
    small children want it, dangle it from small
rods. The perch is a fish made for going
    barefoot, for spooling a line into the well
of your earliest dreams. Grown men throw them
    away, rip the swallowed hook with the guts
        and throw the stiffening little fella
    smack onto the water, not caring much—
well, not caring at all if they're real men—
    food for turtles; anyway, war is hell.

This is a world of big dreams. Or are they not
    dreams properly called at all?—but desires,
hot surrenders to what we haven't got,
    a rage of excellent and tragic fire;
for dreams are visions of what we have. Desires
    build empires and dreams endure them. You wake
        to find that you still have the yellow perch
you caught and threw back when you were five.
    The man in you survives whatever hurts;
    it's the dreams, good dreams, that are hard to take—

to wake to them, some nothing's given up.
    Here was a grandpa, not a boy, who caught
a string of perch. At the time, he was hungry
    I speculate, because he kept them all—
a pail of yellow and orange, silvery,
        and decent-sized for perch, a poor man's mess
            for an old Norwegian who seemed to know
that this was his last time fishing. And he
    cleaned them all. Thinking boiling would be best,
        he asked for it done. Flatbread and potatoes—

the hard bread so he wouldn't feel the bones—
    because perch are full of bones—and the spuds
because they go with fish. Four quiet souls
    sat at table, and Martin ate them up—
the perch, that is, and only half of them,
    picking like a tinker, bent close, half blind,
        mouthful after mouthful of little bones,
masticating them with the muddy flesh
    on principle, nothing wasted, alone
        this time in our sight, Signe irked, Art kind

    and grandson Kent swallowing his first grief
        with his fried sunfish. Grandpa had enough
long after the others, whose dull relief
        did him nor them any good. He said "Uff!"
and worked to his feet, heroic as Christ
        but for no one. And here we are, as mortal
            as he was but only half as Norwegian
and not yet run out of hopeless desire.
            Let us cross the river and go back to our dreams.
            Let us lie down on the mind's grassy shore.

—

And when we wake into that other dream,
        the children will be whole again, more full
            of what's to come than ever they were here—
little fishers dangling golden perch, real
        as dollars: all you have to do is pull
            them in, and they will make you what you are.
And love? All the love you can hold and more,
        the blood of Christ heroic in your veins,
a circulating testament of gore
        without the disillusionment and stains.

And time, inverted, comes from what you will,
    just enough and not too much, as rivers
        carve their courses. There will be no droughts, floods,
dams. Everything you have suffered will heal:
    if that is what you dream. Those who are cursed
        with bad dreams still might suffer something good.
It might be the mirror image of here—
    identical, considered from within,
but treating everything, seen from out there:
    sin soothing virtues, virtues choosing sin.

He will catch the trout I always wanted,
    Grandpa will, perch transfigured into game
        brought in a creel rustic with summer grass
to that great feast of the Kingdom of God—
    not because he wished it, but all the same:
        he awakes, and he wished because it was.
His long lost love will never have been lost;
    for whatever dreadful might here befall,
in the other dream everything is best:
    better to love, and never lose at all.

He goes out fishing on the Rattle Bridge
    and the morning is green in early June,
        vivid as a clean glass bowl of water.
He pulls line from his old reel to the inch,
    exactly right, so a tug on the bobber
        hooks the fish. By God, everything is new!
Even the old reel is perfect, shiny
    silver. God made it himself in heaven,
and all those perch have grown into trout, finely
    poised suspended, graceful in expression,

and the whole morning can't be beat. Twenty
    trout for Ingeborg and the twelve angels
        visiting today, tramps from off the tracks
nearby the house, fresh with stories and plenty
    of soft figs from the hand of David's Michal,
        and pomegranates for the long ride back.
"Come along," they'll say, but Martin says *Takk*,
    no thank you, because it's so pretty here.
Our unborn grandson is learning to walk
    beneath his mind's glassy, cold-handled bier.

—

Everything depends on what you dream. Perch
    can be real when you hold one in your hand;
and memory is a matter of reach.
    The biggest question is not Why but When
because the dreamer sleeps inside the dream,
awakening in good time, a dreamed dream
    in the eternal fisher called the Self.
The one Self is exactly what it seems,
    and also exactly everything else.
    What's a fish but a pretty silver bell

made golden by the attitude of breath
    and caught within the passing human mind?
        It's not a silver bell; it's a fish.
Perch are not trout and nothing dead is best.
    It is one thing to read a Upanishad
    and another to take it for the wind.
But let us go; let us half cross the river
    and fish from the bridge of our memories
rattling while holding mortal ends together—
    cold, golden, grief-stricken as they may be.

The Compleat Angler

Old Isaac Walton pointed out that Jesus,
that time when most he wanted witnesses,
took fishermen along to what would be
the mount of his transfiguration—Moses
and Elijah appearing beside him,
and Jesus' face alight as a vision
of God, robe radiant as a prism
beaming uncreated light—took fishermen,
writes Walton, for they are calm and peaceful,
thus most suitable for revelations,
contemplative, cool—but of course he's full
of wit, and what he doesn't need to say
is fishermen, of all God's creation,

are least likely to let facts bar the way
to truth, so to speak. But to say it plain,
those guys told one hell of a fish story.
Let us go over the lesson again:
they see the vision and say, "Let's build booths,
one for each of you." Ice fishermen. Least
of all fishermen limited by the truth
as responsible humans would perceive
that misconception. The light I believe,
but I think they threw in the booming voice:

"This is my son, listen to him!" The three
made up the voice to give the story sense,
the way a group of misbehaving boys

on whom the future dropped in present tense
would put their heads together and tell one,
explaining the uncanny in defense:
We weren't asleep and we weren't very drunk.
Theologians they were not. All they knew
was that the face of mercy shone like God;
and every fisherman knows that it's true.
But once you have to put it into words
it sounds like the world's most stupendous lie.
Love is best. No dreamer goes to hell.
There is a fish out there for you the size
of Connecticut. Whoppers, I confess,
but true—and I'm a fisherman myself.

thou shalt break them with a rod of iron

It's like dry-fly fishing for trout: casting and back-
casting, endless loops and retreats, whipping and hack-

ing air; stiff shrubs, tree branches overhead except
one clear line perhaps of space that nature may have kept

open for light, and into it, line after line,
pouring all that heavy filament—in time

to some slow metronome of hope inside or out-
side the mind—all that substance in the air; the trout

a guess, hypothesis, a faith, in a cool pool
perhaps, at the end of the bright lane, a jewel

in a blue as limpid as air—if it is there
at all, under that dangerous shade—if there

at all; and now the maximum that can be cast
is curving back—a swan's neck rolling flat—the last

false forward fling having almost licked a white tip
of a hackle of the weightless fly over the lip,

the penumbra, of the focused sphere—the crisp fly
riding toward the center of a vicious eye,

odorless, exact, as unlike hands and brain
as the rainbow in the pool is unlike rain:

now the wrist turns forward in the concentrated
power and surprise of art, line's curve inflated

smoothly up and forward toward the form each cast
has sought and settling forward like a chord. Arrested.

The fly hooked on a twig, the line sags limp onto
the water with a peeling slap. The pool is cold now.

Begin again. Begin again. Pick up the sickly
line and swallow it again. Go forward quickly;

first yourself and then all blessings everywhere
must be sought and broken with the rod you bear.

Pool (Doubt)

A pool might hide the last thing you expect—
a bullhead or a hungry rainbow trout:
our hopes are made to suffer and perfect.

The only light we see is what reflects;
what's underneath the surface is blacked out:
a pool might hide the last thing you expect.

What's risked is either left to soak or wrecked;
you never know until the cast's afloat.
A hope is made to suffer and perfect.

What's hidden, it is wisdom to respect;
the law is for the confident to flout.
A pool might hide the last thing you expect.

Are you among the blessedly elect?
Is certainty superior to doubt?
Our hopes are made to suffer and perfect.

The law is writ in water—what's correct
won't bite you if you never try it out.
A pool might hide the last thing you expect.
Our hopes are made to suffer and perfect.

St. Croix

The St. Croix River is the universe.
There's no freshwater fish that isn't found
somewhere in its hard blue from the Woods down
to where it meets the Father of Waters:
silvers, saugers, catfish, walleye, sturgeon—
anything you'd name that wasn't made up
by anyone but God. As it was said
so long ago, so still it must be said,
"When the Creator poured His pearly cup
of wonders out, He called it the St. Croix."
I said it years ago, and when I'm dead
someone else will say it. And one might say—
possibly I heard it said as a boy—
that if it's not in the St. Croix you don't
need it, and couldn't use it anyway
if you had it. There's nowhere else to fish
but in the universe. Think you're alone
around some secret and secluded bend,
and find we're all fishing in the same hole.
Where the river goes, there must we all go,
Alpha and Omega, world without end,
amen. It must be so; let it be so.

But still, it all started with a great wish
in the dark, and what came out was not dark,
so maybe the next world won't be water
or even air. It's said it will be spirit
but I think it won't be spirit either,
for everything is spirit now; God walks
in a robe of spirit, and God is here
as breath is breath; but who behind the spirit
walks in being as the distant dark sea
wades the river on, does the river know?
And who hollowed the sea with a seamless dream
and a few words of unhearable talk?
How would a river know, whose rock-hewn flow
it doesn't know, and its self-devouring
multitudes perish in each other's grasp?
What we know goes exactly where we know.
Maybe everything we need is here, crowded
like mirrors in the eye of the pike; maybe
not. Maybe what we need from rivers lasts
just so long as boyhood; then the river
moves—then the deep comes moaning round
with many voices and the moon-teared lady
with the waterfall of auburn hair calls.

Your blinding mind has nothing to give her
but the memory of longing you called
the river, that once was everything—
muskellunge and bass, the flaming rainbows
from the northern creeks, bluegills big as hands,
sand bars where you could lay your heart, clear springs
from the Pleistocene, and the starry shadows
on the water summer nights when you called
her believing she called you. Boyhood ends
in a school of perch gold and glistening,
and you know where you think you ought to go.
Then the orange Ulysses says Come my friends,
'tis not too late to seek a newer world.
And the river knows.

The Old Toll Bridge

My home town is a river town. That means
the way I have of understanding life
is rivers—and two particular streams,
not water in general. When one's sight
is channeled by the Willow and St. Croix
you become a flexible, romantic Lutheran,
among some other things. But any boy
would be awed by that beautiful cold blue
that thirty miles down puts its wide might in
and makes the laughing Mississippi
into the Father of Waters Lincoln
said should always flow "unvexed to the sea."

There used to be a toll bridge between Hudson
and Minnesota, the quarter mile out
to the powerful channel from Wisconsin
spanned by banked-up earth and heavy concrete
like a causeway, the rest an iron bridge
with piles driven into the rocky bed,
long gone the way of Pharaoh's pyramids,
the massive labor still in evidence.
At the near end you fish for sunfish, crappies,
silver bass when they're in; and walleye at night:
but out at the deep end it's channel catfish
the size of torpedoes, tremendous pike,

and the goat-ugliest fish in the world,
legendary to Chippewa and Norse,
the size and depth of submarines: sturgeon—
a hundred fifty pounds of scaly force,
scales the size of dinner plates. Caviar
is wrung from some subspecies, but not from these
battle wagons. Thing is, you know they're there.
At the hulk's tug you cut free from the beast.
The channel cats are something else again,
long and strong in that deep wintery flood,
as whiskered and intelligent as men;
they have the North Woods in their limpid blood.

Nowdays the toll bridge is a promenade,
its deep end a little beach in summer
satellited by runabouts and yachts.
A power plant went in up the river,
heated up the water, killed the cold-running
fish; but we always have forever
and there'll always be another summer.
Eternity can stand our bad weather.
By the time you read this, the Asian carp
might have eaten all the old species up,
but there is no end to the love of art,
and God makes rain for the just and unjust.

Still, if I could have my short-sighted way
I'd go back, maybe not for very long,
for at least one good midsummer day.
I'd walk the rough old rocky way, take along
my old pal Mike, and stand out at the end
for a while, make some long and arcing casts
while figuring everything out with my friend.
Of course I've had that good day, and it lasts.
"You can't step into the same river twice":
it stands written by wise and inspired hands.
But Mike has always given good advice,
and there's still a lot left to understand.

Still better than knowing would be simply
being there. Every once in a while you
can sure use a little home. Without trying,
you're bound to lose the one thing that is true:
you. That toll is our only one, fatal
as a hot dam, and the whole universe
depends on getting it back. The latest
Jesus was seen fishing. Vishnu's one birth
is continual. I'd never say so
to his face, but Mike's every bit as true
as the St. Croix. Ask the angels: they know
their Song of God. They know Krishna is blue.

When you have lost a bay horse, hound, and dove,
the best thing you can do is find a good
river and go fishing. You can try love,
you can try peace, goodwill, and brotherhood;
but I recommend fishing. Seek ye first
the Kingdom of God and all these other
things shall be added unto you. The worst
thing you can do is lose your childhood's trust
in the only God you have seen face to face.
The river comes down with the snow and cold rain;
in the summer it rests, and with age flows away.
At the end of all things it arises again.

The Town

A river makes glad the City of God
and Hudson has two. Up along the ridge
overlooking the St. Croix mounds of sod,
tombs of timeless people, watch the new bridge
that will not last long. The sun goes down there
with ancient respect, ceremonial,
as partial to that place as the pine air.
The sun rises over Trout Brook and only
there, decreed from ages past to follow
that mild and winding hallelujah blue,
blessing the heads of fishers on the Willow
widening to all truth in Lake Malilieu.
Let them praise it further who love it most—
the modest rivers, sun, and Holy Ghost.

The Northern Pike

Some think the Northern Pike is not a fish
but something in the family of fire.
They have seen everything they know perish;
they have had visions; they have been devoured.
Those less prescient call it a wolf in armor—
tyrant, predator, pure malicious harm
with teeth on tongue and palate. But the Vedas
know better. One of them, now lost, was called
the *Minnehabhrata*, which scholars dated
earliest, and was wisest of them all.

This Veda placed the end of all things first,
for all has come from nothing: the pure light,
whose risk we are, whose elementary burst
sustains our breath, arose from Elder Night—

the house of Shiva, who wrapped all prior
worlds in nothingness, and from whose veiled hands
the future, darker than the ghost of fire,
comes forth as from a womb. Who understands
death has opened the rose lotus of life—
in other words, has caught a northern pike,
probably in Minnesota. Norwegians
are everywhere, however: in Tibet
the Dalai Lama's understated teachers
roll their lutefisk in lefse, you bet.

Minnehabhrata, written in Old Norse,
was called Song of Shiva, Opening Day.
My reconstruction is far from its source,
but it's better than nothing, anyway.

Shiva's incarnation in this Veda
is a Ganges pike who speaks from an old
fisherman's basket. The man is afraid,
but Shiva's words arrest his quaking soul:
I am Death, the swallower of worlds.
From me comes life, and life to me returns.
From there the Veda opens like the dawn,
and the trembling fisherman is gilded
by its beauty. Now the old man is gone
and the Veda has returned to the wild.

But every pike is death, a swallower
of worlds, an incarnation of Shiva;
for no word of the Eternal is lost,
and every living river is a Veda.

Around the world, the hungry pike is hunted
by the only creature more devouring
than he: a creature who swallows the sun,
who eats the sacred kine of Brahma raw,
the final incarnation of terror
who bleeds the very air with his power,
who turns the lakes and rivers into dust
and draws leviathan out with a hook,
puts an end to the unjust and the just,
writes it down in the last, lost Domesday Book.

We are become Death, devourer of worlds,
hunter and killer of divine Shiva,
who sang an imperishable Veda
in the last perishing universe.

The Worm

The worm is a small word that crawls from one
side of the mind to consciousness, pushing
against the crumbling finitude of earth.
If your soul is the soul of an angler,
you might hope that word will catch a big fish—
The Meaning of Life, The Presence of God,
or Happiness; but you know past all doubt
that you have all three in fishing itself,
even if you can take no trophy home—
that is, away from the time spent angling.

As such, the worm leaves much to be desired
as symbol or synecdoche for death,
its force and work being so opposite
to giving up under dark circumstances.
He feeds on death, but so does poetry;
and if a better metaphor for verse
is found tomorrow I will honor it
the best way I know how: by writing it
on water. The poet and the fisher
both brood over the face of the waters
and leave their presence written tenderly.

The water takes it all in; but the word
was with God, and the word was God. The worm
begins more modestly, but also makes
a universe from nothing you and I
would recognize as universe: garden
from granite, Atlantis from dust, and dust
from hydrogen and iron. And he never
gives up. When you and I ask if it's all
worthwhile, there he goes as usual, blitz-
fast compared to all the death around him.
Perhaps the worm's not words but the poet,
beside whom we writers are mere artistes.

Words make up our world of meaning
but the worm gulps through it cavalierly
at our death, leaving something utterly
different yet completely familiar.
Anyone who can do this is clearly
on top of things. What exhilaration
for anyone possessing a central
nervous system. But the lowly angle-
worm proves himself to be above it all,
devoting himself to meditation
and working out his own slow salvation.

The worm, he works from prose to poetry
and nudges mountains bit by bit for rhyme—
to what avail is difficult to see
but he builds the earth. It isn't easy.
Starlight is much harder than it seems,
dropping off a ball of granite and iron
right here, and telling the worm, "Make it home."
Root, hog, or die, you might say. "And your name
is worm," the starlight adds. But he endures,
worm does, and shoulders through inert eons
slow as vision, but every bit as sure.

Hail to thee, creature with a Latin name!
Caesar had one, Aurelius and Virgil
too. *Lumbricus terrestris*! Conqueror,
stoical philosopher, and poet,
thou Zen-like representative of time,
of death and resurrection, always working
like a hermit measuring vast empires
with thy body, a humble lyricist
sifting continents for a perfect rhyme,
evidence the world's a palimpsest,
a masterpiece gradual and sublime!
Thou provest that whatever is, is best.

All the worm's humility and patience
surely show the rest of us how to live—
building for the soul more stately stations,
ever humbler: a fertilizing sieve,
himself a banquet for a hungry world!
If fish can symbolize a son of God,
then worms symbolize ambrosia, hurled
like manna for fish from bluegills to cod,
and food for thought for that divine offspring,
us. Only Jesus, the divine orphan—
abandoning himself, himself offering,
the sea of stars contracting to a fisherman—
was purer than the necessary worm,
whose firmament is anything but firm.

Bass: An Ode

The bass, the largemouth in particular,
has been unfortunate. In hot summer,
when everything is sullen with the heat
down along the Swanee, the water warm
enough to kill brook trout, expensive reels
click, and bellied men with cupid-leg arms—
posteriors settled on their swivel seats—
flip bacon rinds and popping lures and worms.
Oh, you should see the lunker bass jump then,
their burly bodies flashing for those burly men.

But real fishermen cannot be snobs
who turn their noses at those bass-boat jobs
with motors bigger than the Taj Mahal,
and coolers full of Miller Lite and Bud,
and men with backward baseball caps withal.
Judge not, I say, lest ye yourselves be judged.
"Know that the Self is pure and immortal,"
declares the Katha Upanishad.
Nor disrespect the clueless largemouth bass
who jumps for every blubbery fat ass.

Let the one without sin cast the first stone—
which by the way, a bass would probably bite;
let the lofty connoisseur fish alone—
probably for bass; probably at night:
for every one of us has that within,
perceived or unperceived, we call the Soul.
Every good old boy could be a Brahmin—
if not the wise man, then at least the bull.
For all we know the saints in heaven cast
their crowns to catch the ever-humble bass.

The Beauty Spot

But when it's not the fish, when what you ask
is amplitude and evidence of God,
fall back on beauty, find the place that lasts
in your mind like the only dream you had.
My Signe raised me when a second time
the TB struck my mother, resurrected
me from a cold wet foster crib—not crying,
for I had given up like Lazarus;
and her next miracle was to show me
a place she liked to fish alone sometimes,
a secluded wooded bend where nobody
much bothered, but when the summer sun shines

in that place in my mind, it is a dream.
"The beauty spot" she called it. The Willow
is slow there. She'd take her flyrod downstream
and I'd go up. After an hour or so
we'd meet back where we started, with no fish
but with ticket stubs from Jerusalem.
Sometimes it's not the fish, and all you ask
is resurrection from your lesser wishes,
to wake in beauty, find the place that lasts
and stay there. In this world you can't stay long
in such a place: our great brains run on fish,
and man can't live on amplitude alone.

I would not want to go back there alone,
and doubt that after all these business years
it looks the same. I'm a man, fully grown;
and if you'd ask me, I'm glad to be here
in the fabulous tomb that I have earned
by selling fish. My Signe is somewhere
where the Willow River rises early
and has nothing to do all day. She casts
a lazy line into that ample stream.
She's where it's not the wishes you have asked,
but just the dream that you have always dreamed.
The place of beauty is the place that lasts.

Gone Fishin'

"Deep down in the hearts of most of us, there is just a little loneliness and hunger, which we never quite understand. We are never quite satisfied..."

"... there are so many solemn and significant mysteries to be solved..."

—Charles Elliott, *Gone Fishin'* (1953)

Do not forget. And put away the crystal
   weed of nightshade, hemp, wolf's-bane, rosary
of substances. There is no time. Mysteries
   more solemn than the massive, slow, stately
split and fall of glaciers to warming seas
   are here for us to solve in one short life.
     These unknowables are joy's soft passing-bells.
The first is Longing's dark nativity,
   for once she is born nothing's ever quite
     right, enough, or sufficient in itself.

Where has she come from and why was she born
    in us at all? She is our own angel
whose hand is always at our brow at dawn,
    touching sweet anguish that prompts us to awake.
The question's in rain dimpling a trout stream
    and pattering on luminous new leaves
        one ominous fresh morning in late May.
It has the airy thinness of a dream
    that gives you hope even as it bereaves.
        It is faithful: it never goes away.

You try to beat it senseless on the streets,
    prosper it to death, just grow out of it,
settle. But you are in love with beauty,
    and what you have lost you will not forget.
So anything but this pain is a fool's
    game. This is what the waiting is, the hope
        and even the faith in melancholy,
your ridiculous fly over a pool—
    your stupid line as fat as a ship's rope,
        thinking maybe this one's eternity.

"Here lies one whose name was writ in water."

I'd fish with Mr. Keats if he would fish with me.
Although there aren't many bad fishermen,
you must chose well when fishing for eternity.

He wrote his name in water: that is poetry
and fishing. John Keats was a fisherman.
I'd fish with Mr. Keats if he would fish with me.

In this world there is no surplus of sanity;
I'd like to have a poet for a friend.
You must choose well when fishing for eternity.

I'd take you with us, too, and we'd go out, we three.
I've learned that love and water never end.
We'd fish with Mr. Keats, if he would fish with me.

We would go out and we would see what we could see;
a chance like that would never come again.
You must choose well when fishing for eternity.

We'd write our names in water—oh, the mystery!—
and talk about it happily in heaven.
You do choose well in fishing for eternity.
I'd fish with Mr. Keats and he would fish with me.

Art and the Big Dam

Art came from Minnesota in the early
Thirties, a farmer' son with as honest
a face and mind as ever graced the prairies
since Lincoln. He came at the very worst
time, the Depression, and there were no jobs
in Hudson except for Recovery Act
work. So he helped build the Big Dam that stopped
the Willow at its mouth, and so made Lake
Malilieu. It took a lot of strong men
to say No to all that water, say Wait—
and Art was a strong man, a Norwegian
on both sides, at such perfect peace with fate
that he never vexed anything. No saint
ever believed less than he in doing what ain't.

"Easy-going" you would say if you know
how to recognize an innocent heart.
Others used to say he was just plain slow.
And some believed he was not very smart:
he didn't care about money at all,
worked as a hand on one of Ward's big farms,
kept a dog for duck hunting in the fall,
owned some clothes, rod and reel, gun, an old car—
and when I knew him he had sold the gun.

The dog was a soldier with ghost-gray eyes—
"Antisocial, you know; but a good one,"
Art told me, not meaning to eulogize
exactly; you don't do that for a hound.
But Art missed the old fellow anyhow,

and had no more desire for duck hunting.
He turned to fishing as his life's desire.
And that's how I knew him those long summers
on the rivers. His sun-burnt auburn hair
was salted gray by then, and his hunchback—
"physiology is fate," of one kind—
was noticed more the more spare he became;
but he honored the Brahma of his mind
and lived like a man who had earned his name.
Who better to bind a willowy stream
to a sculpted lake whose musical spray
still becomes rainbows? So the rolling cream
where the Willow pours into the St. Croix
became a faultless prism for a boy,

perfectly splitting his faith, hope, and love
into something he can understand: fishing.
Of course vaster ends ordained from above
were served, but to this boy fishing is fishing.
The Big Dam was anything but a curse—
but if it were, "Hell for society"—
and for society one could do worse
than Art. A brief hold on infinity
is a lot of trouble but the beauty
of it lasts. In the hot August dog days
when the sun is a graveyard in the sky,
this is about the only place that pays.
There's not much doing when The Pond is low,
but if you're patient this is where to go.

I don't know what all else Art built, except
himself—what stately mansions he put up
in his mind or what broad Waldens he slept
beside; but I think we may well be judged
by the life we have imagined. All will
be judged by the life we have lived; but more
by the difference between the two. One heals
the other if the two are not at war.
I hope to see the Dam again this summer
and to hell with the No Trespassing
signs. As long as fish still like the water,
you have to allow for fishermen. Cast
across the boundaries of the infinite,
and the Words of Promise are first to bite.

I'll see him there maybe, shuffling hunchbacked
with a fishpole in his hand, puffing clouds
of glory, clambering down the rough track
beside the concrete wall he helped pour, bowed
like the perfect Seraph who divides the Presence
of the Lord with a watery prism,
taking it easy and watching his step.
Will he know the boy he made and christened
a fisherman, or will he pass me by
as blind to memory as the Brahmin
who's seen the sum of all that lives and dies?
I think he'll clap me with a farmer's hand
hard on the shoulder, eyes like morning dew,
and say Let's go on down and catch a few.

Muskie

I hardly believe what I remember,
    though it was not so long ago
and the memory is not so tender
    that I need to doubt what I know.
Still, it is called "the fish of a lifetime"
    for a reason. The poet William Blake
        at age three saw God look in a window,
            the face as true as rhyme,
    and knew no chance of making a mistake,
        never asking himself, "How did I know

it was God?" You don't need to ask: vision
    carries its own confirmation
like the great muskellunge carries the sun
    between its teeth. And that white sun
blinds the sickly, pale hue of later thought
    like a blade drawn across an open eye:
        the way that you can see is not the way.
            You're left with what you caught
    pure—purity itself that purifies
        the waking dream overcasting the day.

One early evening, two of us trolling
    the shoreline of a quiet lake
Up North, I was very loosely holding
    my little spinner from our wake—
on eight pound test line. Something took my hand.
    I didn't see it, but the stone of power
        stopped the world. "Take it easy," my friend said
        and killed the motor. Grand
    is a poor paper word. After an hour
    so it seemed, we saw the fish's head

looking not so much a head as a face,
    all faces, beholding as one,
the way the universe would look from space
    if it were all one blinding sun—
though you weren't blinded and it was a face
    beautiful beyond words and memory.
        You don't see God as God is in that dark
        bright Self—but what is grace
    but the visibly veiled Divinity,
        the farmer's hand on the door of the Ark?

It tore the net with quick and blunt contempt
    and dangled my twisted spinner
from its hard, razor jaw as if it meant
    to have fishermen for dinner.
It looked too steely muscular to float,
    all muskie like a diamond is all gem,
        sides barred with spots of brown and piney green.
        And right there in the boat.
    The Lion of Judah in Bethlehem—
        like a child it breathed, like a sword it gleamed.

Holy Jehovah, gleaming slick and bright,
    did He who made the lamb make thee?
I slid it back, an arc of snapping fight,
    to its watery purity.
You stand in the boat and you hold your breath,
    the bottom a wreck of net, line, and poles,
        with the last evidence pooled on the floor.
        Once face to face with death
    and life, and the Old One looking at your soul,
        you do not see the way you saw before.

That evidence is written in the water
    of language figuring the mind,
the terrible glory nothing but thought.
    What is poetry of the blind?
Where is the image? What else can God do
    but disappear, beautiful once then gone,
        a fleeting music in the brooding deep?
        Imagine what we knew
before we left the syllable of dawn
    to row across this alabaster sleep!

The Ocean

O Goddess!—may I use the word as well
    as any other for the wine-dark sea—
the sea, that far as anyone can tell
    is nothing but the visible Psyche?
The ocean no-one knows—the "vasty deep"
    whose spirits from their uncreated home
we conscious fishermen can call from sleep
    at will, "but will they come?"—
it gave us life, and it has taken life
    in greater numbers than have all the gods.
Even lordly Mars and his luscious wife,
    who measure from their incestuous bed
in the mind our helplessly fated lives:
    they too come from the sea
and swell and settle with its umbrous tides.
I saw the two lying in desire bright
    as rising lava, in high misery—
the hard-muscled god and his writhing bride,
our two parents drunk in the lust of night.
    One, sheer force, whose only mistress is love:
        the soldier-boy I knew;
    the other holy as the brooding dove,
        but is she love?

Call the fatal whaling fields fisheries
    or demons we can diagnose, mad hunts
for death, commercial or literary—
    the whales submerged Arcturus and his sons,
innocent as strawberries until we lance
    them. Sometimes the obsessing mind wants oil.
Sometimes it wants light for its own sake, glancing
    from a jeweled crown: double, double, toil
        and trouble—drill for it
with harpoon javelins thrown from rolling boats
    or half a mile of steel from offshore rigs,
        anything to keep the world lit.
Still death comes out in roiling toxic smoke,
    and thick crude leaks and spreads like a brute Id,
the shadow and the hand of death. We are fools
    and no oracle, no strangulate voice
        of pale-mouthed prophet dreaming,
nothing stops the spreading pool,
    the last marsh herons and glued gulls screaming:
    the world is gone; the mind is its own place.
Cursing the air, the water, and the fire,
the mind wraps itself in ink and retires.

This is how the world ends. The Earth-birthed soul
    runs a crooked pace under heaven's face
        and drops into its own hole,
    the mind the sunken shrine of a damned race,
leaving a wide quietness where the brain
    had a place in the damp animal husk—
and nothing but a rough beast remains
    on the Earth's roasted and cancerous crust.
Too much! and not enough, the ocean rises
    and falls to the round of the mindless moon,
a wash of water, past the last crisis
    of what the mind was once.
    Good night, sweet prince!
May angels you have seen remember you
    while God flits from memory to memory,
on to the next cosmos. So it begins—
    a Dove over the sea—
ark's door ajar to let the judgment in!

The Little Dam

Back then Black people would cross to the dams
where the Willow falls into the St. Croix—
poor folk with angleworms in coffee cans
like ours, but they didn't come here by choice.
Necessity drove them out of the Cities
to compete for panfish with happy white boys,
almost invisibly fishing for dinner.
They are gone but the poor are still with us:
Southeast Asians from the jungle mountains,
a different race of Huckleberry Finns.
They fish not for fight but for flesh and blood.
This is God's country; we eat angels' food
if we own it like proper fishermen.

You'd stand below the Little Dam and see
gossamer lines like spiders' filaments
slanting to the water, relaxed and bent,
coming down gleaming from up in the trees
where Zacchaeus had climbed out of our way,
as I think now, though back then it just seemed
to be what little people did. Those days
we never spoke to each other. We knew
those folks had to fish to live, while we
cast our bobbers like bread, at leisure.
They made life and death of what we laughed to do,

and that ran things a little out of kilter—
them up there silent as the eyes of God
while we were treading where the saints had trod.
There was something of an offense in it.
"You can't fish out a place with rod and reel,"
the lie went, and we knew it was a lie;
we knew that we had sucked the place and thined it
of the fish that ought to be there. So how
could you begrudge them, sitting out of sight
with their sandwiches and glass milk bottles
in their antediluvian quiet,
thick, the old timers used to say, as flies?

There are new old timers now and they talk
about the Hmong people from Vietnam,
who fought and died for our own Uncle Sam—
and some days there's no room to fish at all.
I see an old Hmong grandfather, back bent
with something said by Martin Luther King,
carrying a pail, a rod from Walmart
in his other hand, luminescent heart
dribbling behind him, doing one last thing
before the Southern Confederacy
reads the red codes of the Apocalypse
right, and the sun leaps toward us with a roar.
Then his eyes will become diamonds that see
the writing on the everlasting door.
The winged race-baited worm stirs,
and the sour cup touches the Savior's lips.

A yellow dragon with eyes of an eagle
watches our consciences like the last angel;
the Norse gods have all gone over the dam,
and the wolf is swallowing the sun. Man
in honor sees not, nor does he understand.

Ballad of the Snakehead Fish

I stood upon the old North Hudson bridge
    a fishing rod held loosely in my hand.
The Willow River ran in mud below
    as brown as if it had been land.

The snakehead fish had come from Illinois;
    Wisconsin and the north were out of luck.
The river was a-slither with them now,
    and muddy from their writhing in the muck.

The fish can move on land just like a snake,
    can breathe with lungs as well as gills;
it grows to five feet long and forty pounds,
    and everything it finds it kills.

They have no predators, and eat their weight
    each day with snake-strong heads and randy teeth;
they decimate all fish, amphibians,
    and even water birds, for meat.

They will attack a human being too
    if you should step into their spawn.
I looked across the Willow's slimy grave:
    the world that I still loved was gone.

And then I thought I saw the ghost of Art
    come walk along the railing of the bridge.
"Well, how's things goin'? Catchin' anything?
    You're lookin' pretty disappointed, Kid."

I answered, "All the pretty fish are gone,
    the sunfish and the villanelles,
the sonnets and the blue-green northern pike.
    Pentameter has gone to hell."

I took a breath, then started in again:
    "It used to be that rhythm made a lake,
but now it's all a slur of carp-like eels;
    you never know just where a line will break.

"We catch iambics coated with lead paint;
    the atmosphere is thick with oily fumes.
The Arc de Triomphe's now a Golden Arch;
    they're selling Coke at Napoleon's tomb

and all our manufacturing has gone
    to China, where these ugly fish come from."
"Ayuh," Art said, and spat a squirt of *snuss*;
    "those fish are ugly as they come.

They're like a bowl of greasy worms and eyes,
    and they don't smell so good neither.
I don't like 'em any better than you.
    The way I see it, we got a choice. Either

we learn to like the damn things, stomach 'em,
    or don't go fishin' any more. Or else
could be you got your own idea here."
    I said, "We ought to be true to ourselves.

We fish the way we always have before.
    I wrote a bunch of piscatory odes
in stanzas regular as schools of perch,
    and made them sound like common prose."

"Ya, well," Art said, "just how what you describe
    is better than free verse that lifts your hat
I ain't prepared to say. You know the sonnet
    was invasive once—worked right off the bat

and took over, Eyetalian or no.
    I think it has been rightly said
there ain't an acre on this lovely world,
    or any thought in someone's head,

still in its rightful owner's hands. Maybe
    you're mad because the Japanese—
well no, it's Chinese now—they play our game
    still better than we do." I sneezed

just for the sake of rhyme, and Art caught that
    and said, "See, ain't no particular good
in old ways just for old ways' sake." I said,
    "You mean the beautiful and true are food

to be devoured for profit's sake? These fish
    are Armageddon in our face, but still
they're swarming on the internet, for sale
    or free and everywhere between. They kill

the beautiful and smother out the true.
    I put it that way for the rhythm's sake,
because the two are one, beauty and truth.
    That's what the greatest fisherman would say."

"John Keats? I saw him just the other day.
    He says hello, and don't pay any mind
to anything but your heart's affection,
    imagination's truth, and good strong line."

I looked at where the river used to run
    and when I turned back, Art was gone.
I thought of Coleridge's Ancient Mariner
    who blessed the slithering finned throng

and thereby blessed himself, and wished I could.
    Still even I know there's a lot to love
before the wolf swallows the heavy sun
    and the last lost light falls from above.

Saint Peter was the chosen fisherman,
    and in imagination's holy dream
he saw unclean creatures pour from heaven
    in a scaly, gross, unkosher stream.

"Take up and read!" a voice like music said;
    for we, who've eaten up the globe,
must bless the multitudes, alive and dead,
    before we're given that unspotted robe.

Old Fishermen

I

This was the country of old men. The slow
walking fishermen heavy at the middle,
their steps dragging memories of the Old
Country—quiet husbands and quiet widowers,
out on the bridge before the grainy snow
melted from the banks, looking at the river
while they murmured in dated Norwegian
to the other quiet, lonely old men.

II

An aged man is a forgotten thing,
made of memories that are no-one's now
except his, and his mind is winnowing
old facts from truth, though he does not know how.
He thinks the sad old song, "If I had wings,
I would fly home today." Yes, he would go
where he and the love of his youth were young
and that sad song did not call to be sung.

III

Hvis jeg hadde vinger—wings, then he would
go, carrying his age on his bowed back.
The strong warmth of the new sun would feel good
in his tired bones, and this gravity-thick
body would grow light, and his slow old blood
would turn to light over the Atlantic:
then he would glide in the fullness of day
over the westernmost fjord of Norway.

IV

That is where the summer leaves are made of gold,
and no gleaming things in America
are like them. Nothing invented and sold
lasts forever like the low geese in the fall
flying fast together over the Glomma
River, where in winter the perfect snow
lay softly underneath eternal trees
and we ran together on silver skis.

V

This country is twilight and old with grief,
but memory gives gleam to the shadows
and there is a promise in what we see
with the heart no matter what old age knows.
There is a country pure as memory
where a river royal with salmon flows,
and the great good king Olaf Tryggvason
laughs at what is passing, past, and to come.

Fishing Pals

A long time afterward, say forty years,
I went out fishing with my old friend Mike.
He has a cabin now beside a lake
up north, a boat, some gray around the ears
and a grandson—a little pal of two
who handles anything pronounceable
with the curt absolutist confidence
of a duke. Both of us have lost a few
in life, too understood to mention,
as quiet claimants wear their proper crowns—

like anyone our age. A miracle
is something true that falls onto your way
and gives you back an honest childhood faith,
like an old fishing pal who takes you back
and somehow knows you haven't forgotten.
Where has the time gone and where are the years
a guy might want to ask; but they're right here
like a maple leaf floating on the water.
Eternity is simple. You can stare
at it like a floating plastic bobber

or you can fish for it with wounded faith,
certain in a modest, wry sort of way
that the fish are down there. Maybe today
faith will pay off; if not faith, then practice:
but either way the main thing is to know
it isn't about the fish. Two old pals
sit in the summer center of it all
like dukes—bright sky above, sweet deeps below,
perfectly at home in the long sunshine,
eternal in the oldest, best of times.

Indolence

"Consider the lilies of the field, how they grow. They toil not..."

I'd like to think I had a vision once.
    When Art retired, sometimes he'd rent a boat
and we'd go out on what was called The Pond
    and fish all day. Back then what I liked most
was pulling on the oars. It made me strong,
    I thought; I was kind of in a hurry
        to grow up. It wasn't to be a man
I wanted so much as just to get on
    with whatever I was supposed to try
        in life, whatever I was meant to earn.

But the fishing was good, too. Out all day
    in the sun and that boat rocking a little,
so little you hardly felt it dip and sway;
    nothing in all the world to do but sit
and watch your bobber on the blue water,
    a cusp of red and white that in the shine
of light would disappear altogether
    now and then. You'd see nothing but white line.
It felt like the summer would never end,
and you could always come out and do it again.

A few years later Art cut grass all day
    once a week down on what was called The Point—
shady lawns spread across a few lazy
    acres on the water. One day I joined
him, though not to work. While he thought and mowed,
    I sat. I had worked sixty hours a week
        that college year so I took the summer
off. It had been a hard year and it showed
    in the way I wanted to do nothing
        and called it marching to a different drummer.

I hadn't worked hard enough to avoid
    the sight of death. The country was at war
too, and it made killers out of poor boys
    and brought them home in bags. I sat and saw
the still blue water of The Pond, the far
    shore deep green with the dappled shade of trees.
    I could hear a robin walk. And I knew
everything was one. This is what we are.
    Nothing matters less than what you reason
        out for everybody, or what you do.

Art has been gone and I have studied war
    for many years now, and I have written
the merest poetry; and what I saw
    and felt and knew that summer afternoon
has never come again. But I still go
    fishing when I can and look for it. Art
        is not a substitute exactly, but
sometimes it reminds me of what I know.
    Nothing touches that old firm certainty
        except the measured warmth of poetry

and the loss of eternal ambition
    given to solitudes by humble love—
absolute indolences of vision,
    the Holy Ghost walking in a green robe.
Let us cross over the river and rest
    under the shade of the trees. Let us say
        that Earth is the only place for heaven,
and watch from whatever summer is best—
    wherever this is the only day
        there ever was, and we were together.

Willow River Cemetery

1

The lilac May and clover June of boyhood,
    summer endless in its expectation,
catch in the throat, can't possibly be good
    for a man caught in a dying nation
and trying to figure out how to live
    somewhere between what might have been and what
        the God of Battle knows. If what will come
is just—though I find it hard to believe
    Justice could be not only blind but dumb
for so long, a witness to what is not

rather than what is—but I was saying
    before important prophecy broke in:
childhood is where we can't afford to stay
    if we are serious about our sin
and the sin of others. What's gone is gone,
    because memory is a palimpsest,
        a Grecian urn with a new scene painted
    continually on its clay-brained breast,
a self-serving vanity all along,
    only its soft, soft ash inside untainted.

Truth is a cemetery like the one
    above the little town, a friend to man
but inarticulate and helpless, stone
    dead, stone after stone and one fisherman,
one soldier, one grandfather after another;
    a resting-place of tuberculosis,
        influenza, battle wounds, and bad luck;
beside one mother, another mother,
    childhood after childhood an erased book,
and everyone's story a mortal's guess.

The cemetery's fishermen caught fish;
    their wives cooked them, their children ate them—here
they lie. It was a fine thing to have lived.
    The immigrant with his Ingeborg near,
so near and still: the sun was in her sighs
    once, that we know: and she was beautiful
        to him, we are certain, as childhood's certain
and as childhood's irrefutably wise;
    and as fish rise to patient fishermen,
so love comes by whatever chance it will.

And the old town goes as the town will go,
    a river in the summer sun. Beneath
its shady green and flowing trees it knows
    all that it needs to know. If its last truth
is its own beauty, and all its memories
    must be surrendered to a world of clay,
        let it be. Let its summer never cease,
let what it once was be what it will be,
    and let its rivers carry it away.
        It is fine to have been loved, and at peace.

2

The man who named the cemetery was
 a fisherman and had a poet's heart—
it's said that fishing is as fishing does
 and naming is an act, a work of art:
witness the names set in stone here. They're all
 that's left of these lives, or so it would seem—
  names and the defiant, flowery ways
their survivors (you'd like to say "so-called")
 carved bold notice of their love or esteem
  on stones protesting these horrible graves.

No one except the antiquarians
 visits the old section across the street:
the founders, settlers of the early town.
 Their graves are gentle, melancholy, sweet
for being unseen. But here what you see
 first thing is a row of military
  graves, Civil War dead, the misty young men
who marched in the Republic's Grand Army—
 decorated on Decoration Days
  years ago. My mother remembered them,

old white-haired stooping men, already far
    away, long ago and far away, canes
pressing grass by graves—comrades of their war.
    They saw Lincoln, Grant. You can read their names.
Behind them in an attitude of rest
    but active in decay, the universe's
        poor. All they have is our best wishes.
We hope they're with God—safe, contented guests,
    swingers of the Twenty-third Psalm's birches.
        Wouldn't it be nice if they've all gone fishing.

Why is it—this strange sensation of peace
    here? No despair or easy cynicism
dispels it. You walk by the graves and each
    one imparts a kind rest that no sleep gives
and no faith's assurance can counterfeit.
    Only fishing does it. Why? The unknown
        lives below the water's reflecting face
perfectly made, a trout. You can seek it,
    or not. There's no rest in what's not your own.
        Fishing, you are somehow learning your place.

These old soldiers knew one kind of glory
    without knowing it. Duty is a word
for the future. To sense eternity
    is to be teased from thought; and to have heard
the beauty of this silent river, Willow
    River, is to go where the naming mind
        must be silent, where the epitaph read
is written on the waters. The heart knows
    the names of all these unreflecting dead,
    and knows the truth of beauty to be kind.

The Willow River at Night

You find along the way, and pretty late
    along the way, that what you did was wrong—
oh, years ago, and hidden from your sight,
    and you have ignored it for way too long.
Your children carry your error like genes
    and life has no pity on them at all
        for what you did or were too raveled up
in yourself to do. Mute soldiers they fall
and fall all their lives, bleeding like Marines
    on tideless beaches of Guadalcanal,
        not what they could have been. You were their luck.

So you go down to the river tonight
    not to ask forgiveness but to be stunned
somewhere, a place once beautiful and right,
    where you deserved to be out in the sun.
You used to fish here, before the planting
    and the unthinkable stomach-turning
        harvest you have finally understood.
The hard and bright track of a low moon slants
    across the mile-long Pond, coldly burning
like a dropped staff or a broken Commandment.
        God made the world, and saw that it was good.

Then He put it in your hands and stood back.
    Didn't He know? Of course He knew. Then why?
An old rowboat on the bank is a wreck
    of broken, mossy planks. "If a man die,
shall he live again?" The Savior answers
    like water but the old boat is still shot
        and the owl repeats your name like clockwork.
If this moody river rises somewhere
    else the lambs in the channel don't know it.
    Whatever we have made of what is not
        breaks like little waves on the moon-bound earth.

You could stay all night feeling sorry for
    yourself. The owl sounds like she's in the mood
for it, and the little waves could sound more
    like uselessness than the glory of blood.
But you have to believe a little. Not
    so much that you might as well not believe
        at all; just enough to see things. Believe
as though no lives depend on it. It is not
    the Bible tells me so but the river:
    follow it back to what all things once were
and you find nothing, but the nothing was hot.

If you believe nothing but the holy
    affections of the heart, and the plain truth
of the imagination, you believe
    in everything: believe in ghosts and fools,
that this is the afterlife before which
    all of heaven gasped in expectation—
        for dreams were invented here, finally,
though for the longest time they were God's wish
    for us, as were these moon-begotten trees,
    the iridescent and conjunctive eyes
that see them, and the deep forgotten sun.

The moonlight that reflects has come from farther
    than the moon. The moon means you can go home
again: its path on the water is harder
    than it looks. The owl is the snowy soul
and the river is your self. The soul sings
    over the self from the tree of desire.
        This is why you are here tonight. Illusion
has parted like a pair of dying wings
    and you see that the great grand total sum
    of everything is the round number one.
The heart of hearts is less sorry than wise.

The river looks as gentle as the soul
    but is a mirror of the summer sky,
dark as a velvet-lined box of jewels,
    a sparkling windy dust with one cold eye.
It is full of fish; you know it. Imagine
    them fanning gravity slowly, asleep;
        and it is about time the owl sleeps too
where you'll no longer hear her. You're a sage
    on the night grass, the fishes' fool but deep
        with ghosts, for what are the trees if not sweet,
            and what is heaven if it is not you?

*

Someone is watching you, you can be sure—
    a lady or a son who loves you, cool
as night air to the touch, than love more pure,
    invisible as the lotus's jewel—
but watching over you with the pity
    of the dead. Really you do see her but
        you don't believe it. You see her all day
but you believe the sun-glaring city
        instead, philosophy played straight and saved
        from the moon and the river: you can pray
    this philosophy and it will hold up.

But here she is and you know it. You feel
    the past as presence and that's how you know—
or would know if you were not so old. See
    her face and the many with her! But no,
this night river is too long to predict
    and has come from somewhere too tight for ghosts—
        a sunlit spring up near New Richmond maybe,
and not from Indra's engendering hip.
    But He Who Leads the Waters is not old
        enough to think of in theology,
        Eternal Child of the Virgin Mary.

You know, you have seen ghosts like silver leaves
    nearly every day of your life, silver
snow in winter, and silver fish between
    bluegills and yellow perch on wet stringers
in deep summer—always there and you see
    them with your eyes but not your thinking mind.
        They are here now. What do you think you are?
Old friend, where are all of your memories?
    Where is the old surprise of your last war,
        and where is the sharp steel under that scar?
    The ghosts are here and most of them are kind,

  intent to go with you to the mountain
    in the faded old picture on your wall—
  where all the waters of the earth flow down,
    and all the paths come from. They see your soul
  through all these trees and behind all these dreams,
    and where you are going, they too will go.
      Most of them love you. They were sent from above—
  from that same mountain's blue, eternal peak,
    and what they know, some day you shall know.
    So shall I. I suspect we know it now.
      None are so blind as those who will not love.

The land along the river is called Beulah,
  Married, somewhere in the mind of God, green
with summer. Sheer memory takes us there,
  though the crossing is terrible and deep,
as love is. Doesn't it feel better now
  to sit beside this river in the dark
    and count the blessings of mortality?—
its desperation, Keats's burning brow,
    its morose irresponsibility,
  with that full-laden, ever-circling Ark,
  its last dove spent, the many-voiced heart.

*

Are all our loves too dear for our possessing,
    that sure as current all of us return
to the river?—as if it were the best thing
    imaginable, to desert the sun
for a night that lasts until we are born
    again: into absolute nothingness,
or God, or heaven, or another round
        on earth. The Willow flows to the St. Croix
    and we can't hold her to our sinking breast
        for long. The tender night from where we lie
slips eastward as the stone-lidded world turns.

Couldn't we love a little less and keep
    whatever it is and still be human—
still be souls, feel a secure joy, if need
    be grieve short absences, live like the sand
on the moon? But Earth is so beautiful
and blue, a dear light to the blowing universe.
It is what we are, for better or worse,
in sickness and in health, both rich and poor.
    Let us hope that we come around again
and not alone, youthful as a green tree
in the house of the Lord, immortal seed.

But hope is for the fishermen, and not
    for you, you tired and despondent dreamer
sleeping in the only dream you have got.
    Why not wet a line tonight? The fish sleep
with their eyes open, you know. Why not put
God to the test?—a devil's question but
    always allowed to fishermen for free
        because we are beggars, as Luther said
when he was lying by this river—hook,
    line, and sinker in the gracious stream
        that flows from Beulah Land to all the dead.

I never want to leave the Willow River.
    What I know of heaven is here. The sun
rises where the Willow springs. Please forgive
    all my talk. You are growing so intent
that I fill the empty spaces foolishly,
    as if words could delay death, or as if
        thoughts could figure it out, make it better
than it evidently is. Let us fish.
    That is all we have left now; let us fish.
        But oh, friend, I see that you are ready;
I see there is a great burden in heaven.

I will go with you! You are the Willow,
and you are Beulah Land; and where you go
    there I am. All Creation is nowhere
        outside your immaculate soul. This earth
of you is the only heaven I know.
    How cold and ocean-like is the night air;
        the warm Earth mothers God and all His works.
Let us cross over the river and rest
    where the clear springs of Jerusalem rise.
They are the Willow's water: its flood crests
    blue under the Great King's immortal eyes.

The Willow River in Heaven

*There is a river, the streams whereof shall make glad
the city of God.*

The mind's a stream we go a-fishing in,
    but once the brain is dead, what dreams may come?
How can the olive tree bloom ever green
    in the house of the Lord without a sun
that blows its helium, dies like a dog,
    implodes to a stone—and all its peoples
        lie down cold in the unremembered dark?
        The mad Greek face of the farthest red star
could eat all of our rational brains raw
    and still fall no less fast and no less real,
        for all our raging Achillean wars.

The brain makes no difference to its own gods,
    who stumble into immortality
wherever logic doesn't like the odds:
    a bowl of tapioca that can see,
and all Imagination sojourns there—
    the lotus flowering on a summer lake,
        some seven woods and seven ages green
    with grief and possibility, soiled Yeats
during the Troubles, the quantum Shakespeare
    fretting both sides an orchestrated stage,
        Homer's throned bones—all in that gnarled, veined brain.

It is our starry course, that multitude
of soft and slippery circuits; we can go
exactly where it goes—we are its fool,
thinking that we know only what it knows:
it is the river of the moon. Its light
must be reflected light, or it was born
from nothing but itself like a lost boy
in a forest. Whatever is, is right
there in that putty, of course dreaming only
of itself, its god's way the only way—
idea of a soul its only soul.

But there is a river, another river.
Don't ask me how I know, because I don't
know. It is the Willow River in heaven,
rarer than time, round as a pearl. It goes
nowhere, for it is nowhere. Lay your line
in it one day; run your warm hand through it;
cup your hand to drink it and remember.
You'll know your grandfather when you get there;
Mother will stroke away what's on your mind—
and your old pal, he's here and you knew it
when you used to fish that sunny river.

The North Hudson Bridge

You always need a bridge. There's always one
more river, and there's always the other
side. When I was growing up in Hudson
a heavy wooden bridge spanned Malilieu
where it narrowed like a Gay Nineties waist,
and the old timers fished its long walkways.
We boys went too with rods and worms, and raced
the old men to the best spots in the sagging
middle. Sometimes older boys would strip down,
descend the maze of timbers and supports,
and dive like arrows. The old men would frown
and move to smoother water, but we'd wish
for those boys' nerve. On summer evenings couples
brought lawn chairs, stood their poles against the rail,
ate apples and sandwiches for supper,
and watched the sun sink into the St. Croix.
Oscar would saunter with his rubber worm,
dangling it for bass I never saw him catch;
Ehrling, on mornings when the sun was warm,
always dunked for catfish with some stinking
ball of dough; but by and large we all went
for sunfish, each of us waiting our own
way: some grandpa's boys running hell-bent
for somewhere always while the old man ignored
them; red-faced Nels, who talked to everyone
and forgot his rod; the high school mooners bored

in ten minutes and offering their bought
nightcrawlers to us; Signe, whose flyrod
tremored with her Parkinson's; thin Millard,
down to get away from his wife, By God!—
you had the legitimate *snuss* chewer;
and the smoker, good as to say, loose liver:
everyone you'll recognize in heaven.
As Mark Twain said, "Met them on the river."
For many years before, my grandfather
had walked that bridge to work in North Hudson
at the busy Northwestern Railroad yard,
and forge in the hot smithy of the nation's
rolling soul the iron wheels and pumping rods
of a people going somewhere. I think
he'd take a fishing pole along. He'd stand
it by the noisy shop's doors, and then sink
into work—the anvil and coal fire.
In late afternoon he'd come back up—take
up his rod and walk back to the long bridge.
I think sometimes he would stay until late
and think of Ingeborg, and maybe talk
to her. What better place than on water,
looking toward the sun, the Willow moving
to meet the big river. Both his daughters
would have been in Minneapolis then,
and he was on his own. Why go home
in a hurry for nothing? Why not stay
awhile, and fish a little. He'd watch alone
on the bridge come November, fishpole still
over the cold deep river, while the sun
went down red behind the barren St. Croix.

I'd stand and watch with him till Kingdom Come
if I could see him meet his love again
on the other side, see him and Ingeborg
touch; if I could see their faces, hear them.
Maybe that's what I go fishing for.
Time's a stream I go a-fishing in,
someone wrote. *One world at a time,* he said.
It's a wide river to infinity,
and if there's a bridge it must be sacred.
Martin was fishing for eternity
and I will fish with him till day is done,
for love's the bridge we go a-fishing from.